Team Building Strategies for IT Managers

Tips And Techniques That IT Managers Can Use In Order To Develop Productive Teams

"Practical, proven techniques that will help you to create highly productive IT teams"

Dr. Jim Anderson

Published by:
Blue Elephant Consulting
Tampa, Florida

Copyright © 2014 by Dr. Jim Anderson

All rights reserved. No part of this book may be reproduced of transmitted in any form or by any means, electronic or mechanical, including photocopying, recording or by any information storage and retrieval system without written permission of the publisher, except for inclusion of brief quotations in a review.

Printed in the United States of America

Library of Congress Control Number: 2014932023

ISBN-13: 978-1495344589

ISBN-10: 1495344584

Warning – Disclaimer

The purpose of this book is to educate and entertain. This book does not promise or guarantee that anyone following the ideas, tips, suggestions, techniques or strategies will be successful. The author, publisher and distributor(s) shall have neither liability nor responsibility to anyone with respect to any loss or damage caused, or alleged to be caused, directly or indirectly by the information contained in this book.

Recent Books By The Author

Product Management

- Product Management Secrets: Techniques For Product Managers To Boost Product Sales And Increase Customer Satisfaction

- Customer Lessons For Product Managers: Techniques For Product Managers To Better Understand What Their Customers Really Want

Public Speaking

- How To Become A Better Speaker By Changing How You Speak: Change techniques that will transform a speech into a memorable event

- How To Give A Great Presentation: Presentation techniques that will transform a speech into a memorable event

CIO Skills

- How CIOs Can Solve The Security Puzzle: Tips And Techniques For CIOs To Use In Order To Secure Both Their IT Department And Their Company

- What CIOs Need To Know About Working With Partners: Techniques For CIOs To Use In Order To Be Able To Successfully Work With Partners

IT Manager Skills

- How IT Managers Can Make Innovation Happen: Tips And Techniques For IT Managers To Use In Order To Make Innovation Happen In Their Teams

- Secrets Of Effective Leadership For IT Managers: Tips And Techniques That IT Managers Can Use In Order To Develop Leadership Skills

Negotiating

- Learn How To Signal In Your Next Negotiation: How To Develop The Skill Of Effective Signaling In A Negotiation In Order To Get The Best Possible Outcome

- Learn The Skill Of Exploring In A Negotiation: How To Develop The Skill Of Exploring What Is Possible In A Negotiation In Order To Reach The Best Possible Deal

Miscellaneous

- Power Distribution Unit (PDU) Secrets: What Everyone Who Works In A Data Center Needs To Know!

- Making The Jump: How To Land Your Dream Job When You Get Out Of College!

Note: See a complete list of books by Dr. Jim Anderson at the back of this book.

Acknowledgements

Any book like this one is the result of years of real-world work experience. In my over 25 years of working for 7 different firms, I have met countless fantastic people and I've been mentored by some truly exceptional ones. Although I've probably forgotten some of the people who made me the person that I am today, here is my attempt to finally give them the recognition that they so truly deserve:

- Thomas P. Anderson
- Art Puett
- Bobbi Marshall
- Bob Boggs

Dr. Jim Anderson

This book is dedicated to my family: Lori, Maddie, Nick, and Ben. None of this would have been possible without their constant love and support.

Thanks for always believing in me and providing me with the strength to always be willing to go out there and be my best for you.

Table Of Contents

LEARNING TO LEAD EFFECTIVELY 9

ABOUT THE AUTHOR 10

CHAPTER 1: THE JOY OF COMPUTER STORAGE TEAMS 15

CHAPTER 2: BUT I DON'T WANT TO WORK WITH YOU! 18

CHAPTER 3: HOW AN IT LEADER CAN MANAGE COMPETITIVE AROUSAL IN THEIR TEAM 22

CHAPTER 4: HOW CAN AN IT LEADER CHANGE AN ENGINEER INTO A TEAM PLAYER? 26

CHAPTER 5: DO YOU WANT TO WORK WITH AN IT TROPHY KID? 30

CHAPTER 6: AN IT MANAGEMENT NIGHTMARE: MANAGING TROPHY KIDS 33

CHAPTER 7: MANAGING TROPHY KIDS: CAN'T WE ALL JUST GET ALONG? 37

CHAPTER 8: GROUP DECISIONS CAN BE THE WRONG DECISION FOR IT LEADERS 40

CHAPTER 9: ALTERNATE REALITY GAMES: GAMES THAT IT LEADERS KNOW HOW TO PLAY 44

CHAPTER 10: CHEAP & EASY IT MANAGEMENT: HOW TO USE SOCIAL-NETWORK ANALYSIS TO BOOST TEAM PERFORMANCE 48

CHAPTER 11: GOOGLE'S LESSONS FOR MANAGING TECH-SAVVY TEAMS 54

CHAPTER 12: TOMORROW, TOMORROW, YOU'LL ALWAYS HAVE TOMORROW – BUT ARE YOU READY? 59

It Takes A Team...

In order for any IT manager to be a success, the team that you are managing has to learn how to work together. All too often what IT managers don't realize is that your team may not know how to work together and they are going to need you to show them how to do this.

Team building is a soft skill that too many of us have never had any training on how to grow and cultivate. It starts with understanding that every member of your team is an individual. This means that you're going to have to deal with team members who don't want to work with each other as well as members who are locked into destructive competition with each other.

As though that wasn't enough for you to have to deal with, in the modern workplace there are multiple generations working together. One of the greatest challenges that you'll be facing is discovering how to manage the millennial generation – the so-called trophy kids. You need them to be a part of your team, but in order to get them to be an effective part of your team you are going to have to discover how they want to be managed.

Managing in the 21st Century means that social media tools are available to help you connect with your team. You'll need to be careful how you use them, but these tools can help you to bring your team together into a single functioning unit.

The good news is that the solution to building teams is not something that you have to dream up all by yourself. Other firms have faced the same set of challenges and you can learn from them by studying both what has worked for them as well as the things that have not worked for them.

Once you are able to get your IT team to work together, you'll need to be careful to make sure that you are not affected by the downside of teams. Make sure that group decision making doesn't cause you team to veer off into the wrong direction.

This book has been created to provide you with the soft skill training that you are going to need in order to effectively build teams. The goal is to use the skills and talents that each member of your team brings to the table in order to build a high performance team.

For more information on what it takes to be a great IT manager, check out my blog, The Accidental IT Leader, at:

www.TheAccidentalITLeader.com

Good luck!

- Dr. Jim Anderson

About The Author

I must confess that I never set out to be a CIO. When I went to school, I studied Computer Science and thought that I'd get a nice job programming and that would be that. Well, at least part of that plan worked out!

My first job was working for Boeing on their F/A-18 fighter jet program. I spent my days programming fighter jet software in assembly language and I loved it. The U.S. government decided to save some money and went looking for other countries to sell this plane to. This put me into an unfamiliar role: I started to meet with foreign military officials and I ended up having to manage groups of engineers who were working on international projects.

Time moved on and so did I. I found myself working for Siemens, the big German telecommunications company. They were making phone switches and selling them to the seven U.S. phone companies. The problem was that the switches were too complicated. Customers couldn't tell the difference between one complicated phone switch from another complicated phone switch. Once again I found myself working with the sales and marketing teams to find ways to make the great technology that the engineers had developed understandable to both internal and external customers.

I've spent over 25 years working as an senior IT professional for both big companies and startups. This has given me an opportunity to learn what it takes to manage and IT department in ways that allow it to maximize its output while becoming a valuable part of the overall company.

I now live in Tampa Florida where I spend my time managing my consulting business, Blue Elephant Consulting, teaching college courses at the University of South Florida, and traveling to work with companies like yours to share the knowledge that I have about how to create and manage successful IT departments.

I'm always available to answer questions and I can be reached at:

Dr. Jim Anderson
Blue Elephant Consulting
Email: jim@BlueElephantConsulting.com
Facebook: http://goo.gl/1TVoK
Web: **www.BlueElephantConsulting.com**

"Unforgettable communication skills that will set your ideas free…"

Create IT Departments That Are Productive And A Valuable Asset To The Rest Of The Company !

Dr. Jim Anderson is available to provide training and coaching on the topics that are the most important to people who have to manage IT departments: how can I build a productive IT department (and keep it together) while at the same time providing the rest of the company with the IT services that they need?

Dr. Anderson believes that in order to both learn and remember what he says, speakers need to laugh. Each one of his speeches is full of fun and humor so that what he says "sticks" with everyone.

Dr. Anderson's CIO SkillsTraining Includes:

1. How to identify and attract the right type of IT workers to your IT department.
2. How to build relationships with the company's senior management in order to get the support that you need?
3. How to stay on top of changing technology and security issues so that you never get surprised?

Dr. Jim Anderson works with over 100 customers per year. To invite Dr. Anderson to work with you, contact him at:

Phone: 813-418-6970 or
Email: jim@BlueElephantConsulting.com

Blue Elephant Consulting

Speaking. Negotiating. Managing. Marketing.

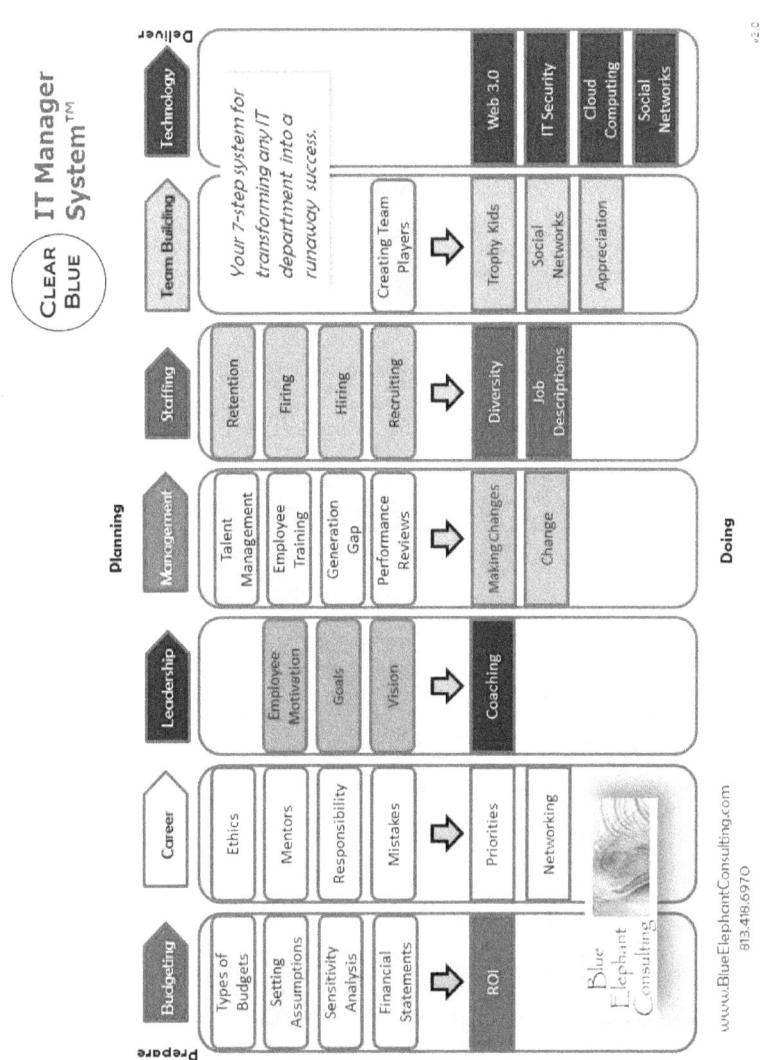

The **Clear Blue IT Manager System™** has been created to provide IT managers with a clear roadmap for how to manage an IT team. This system shows IT Managers what needs to be done and in what order to do it.

Chapter 1

The Joy of Computer Storage Teams

Chapter 1: The Joy of Computer Storage Teams

Recently I had the good fortune to attend an EMC World tradeshow. If you've never heard of this one, then you probably aren't a part of the world of computer storage. EMC is a $15B company that grew large by providing the storage that Yahoo, Google, the government, etc. use to store each and every bit of information that they manage. The tradeshow was a real eye opener for me.

I dabble in the world of storage only when I have a need. The folks who I talked to at the show, on the other hand, REALLY get involved in storage on a daily basis. There were about 9,300 folks attending this show (see — I told you that it was a big deal).

What I observed about this mass of IT professionals is that they all seem to be engaged and motivated. Now I can't say what will happen when they get back to the shop, but at least for the few days that they were out in the desert they seemed to be satisfied with their jobs as well as their companies. If only you could capture this feeling and bottle it!

How did they get this way? I think that it has a lot to do with the simple fact that they are among peers who share the same technical knowledge that they do. This allows them to remember that they are not alone. It also helps that EMC spends the entire show telling them that they are important parts of their company and that the future rests on their shoulders.

Perhaps this type of environment can be captured and used back at home. Within your firm is there any way to set up a birds-of-feather group for technical professionals who share the same types of knowledge but who don't normally have an opportunity to work together? Be careful that this doesn't turn into a complaint club, but if managed and directed, it can become a powerful reason why IT workers join and then don't leave your company.

Chapter 2

But I don't WANT to Work With You!

Barriers to Collaboration

Chapter 2: But I Don't WANT To Work With You!

In an edition of the Communications of the ACM, Peter Dennine and Peter Yaholkovsky discuss an interesting topic: just how do you get a group of people to stop thinking about "me" and start thinking about "we"? They were talking in broad generalities; however, it did get me thinking about how this can be accomplished in IT departments & teams.

Messes are defined as large, complex, problems that appear at first glance to be unsolvable. Really big messes have a special name: "wicked problems". Dennine & Yaholkovsky point out that the only way to solve problems like this is through the use of collaboration.

Collaboration is defined as a working together synergistically. Here in the 21st century, this should be easy to do, right? We've got blogs that talk about important things, wikis, IM, and cell phones. How hard could this be?

Well, it turns out to be quite hard. Most of the collaboration tools that we have turn out to be pretty poor at enabling collaboration. Things got even more complicated when researchers did some testing and found out that you and I don't really like to collaborate.

When we are working on a wicked problem in a group setting, we first like to use authoritarianism, then competition, then finally collaboration. Researcher Nancy Roberts says it best when she said "People fail into collaboration."

So why do we do this? Two guesses: first, we seem to think that we can win in every negotiation by standing our ground. Secondly, we have a hero culture – we look for a hero to rise and solve the problem. If they solve it, they'll get the credit so why make the effort because you're not going to get any credit.

In IT we seem to encounter more than our fair share of "wicked problems". What can we do to encourage collaboration within IT teams when our very nature resists it? If we adopt a three stage process for dealing with wicked problems, we can solve them together: design, collaborate, and follow-through.

The design stage simply requires us to identify all of the affected parties and what questions that they need to answer. Hosting a meeting where a moderator leads the team through a series of follow-through steps can cause collaboration to occur. Basically, you want to state the problem, have everyone discuss it, have folks start to throw out ideas, and then when people start to refine the ideas offered by others, that's when you'll see the real collaboration start to happen.

The authors finish up by asking one last intriguing question: how far up can you scale this approach to solving wicked problems? They've shown that it can work in groups of 50-200 people. The open question is if it can be scaled up beyond that. From an IT perspective, it doesn't matter because that size works well with departments or specific project teams.

In the end, collaboration happens when a team or department comes together to create a solution to a wicked problem that takes care of everyone's concerns at the same time. It sure sounds like we should be trying to make this happen just a little bit more often!

Chapter 3

How an IT Leader Can Manage Competitive Arousal in Their Team

Chapter 3: How an IT Leader Can Manage Competitive Arousal in Their Team

It's great to have an IT team that is full of go-getters. However, as with everything in life, sometimes teammates can be too competitive. When we let the heat of battle overcome our better judgment, then we've got a real problem.

When this happens, we stand a very good chance of starting to make very bad decisions. Long after the competition has been resolved; we will still be living with the effects of those decisions and that can come back to haunt us over and over again.

It has been said that rivalry, time pressure, and a bright spotlight of public attention can all contribute to making us become competitively aroused. This is how we start to make bad decisions. Given all of this, now let's spend some time talking about what can be done by IT leaders to manage competitive arousal within their teams.

An IT leader can work to prevent problems by minimizing the potential for competitive arousal to occur in the first place by doing two things: avoiding the certain types of interaction that can lead to competition among teammates, and working to defuse the common risk factors that can lead to excessively competitive behavior.

In the first case, an IT leader needs to have the ability to think like a chess master and look into the future. He/she is looking to identify those interpersonal dynamic conditions that could lead to competitive arousal within their team.

Once an IT leader has spotted these potentially volatile conditions, then they can step in and can work to restructure the deal making process into one that they believe will still lead to a successful outcome while not leading to an overly competitive situation.

Additionally, an IT leader needs to be constantly working to defuse the risk factors that may lead their teammates to enter into competitive arousal. There are three ways that this can be done:

- **Reduce Potential Rivalry:** Luke Skywalker was motivated to overthrow the Empire at all costs because he saw it as being "evil". When IT workers start to view rivals as being "bad", or "evil" they can start to view winning as being required no matter what the cost. When this happens, the IT leader needs to identify who is feeling the greatest amount of rivalry and then limit their role. Another helpful approach is to do your homework before the competition begins. Clearly lay out how much you are willing to "lose" in order to "win". Doing this before competitive arousal kicks in ensures a more rational decision will be reached.

- **Slow Down The Clock:** In order to reduce the pressure that a ticking clock brings to the table, an IT leader needs to search for ways to stop the clock or at least to extend its window of time. Deadlines are almost always too short in which to complete the work. Extending or eliminating them is a key IT leader job.

- **Dimming The Public Spotlight:** A great way to take the burden of meeting public expectations off the shoulder of individual IT staffers is to spread the decision making responsibility across multiple members. This isn't a perfect solution, but it goes a long way towards reducing the stress felt by individual team members.

Although it's not often that the IT leader is the one who is getting caught up in a competitive situation, he/she does play a key role. The ability to anticipate that a member of the department is going to enter into a rivalry situation, come under time pressure, or get caught in a spotlight is part of an IT leader's job.

In the end, we all overestimate just how rational, careful, and even logical that we are in high pressure situation. It's the role of an IT leader to save us from making bad decisions when we find ourselves there.

Chapter 4

How Can an IT Leader Change and Engineer Into a Team Player?

Chapter 4: How Can An IT Leader Change An Engineer Into A Team Player?

At my core, I am an engineer. I recognize this, I accept this, I am proud of this. However, during my career many mentors have been kind enough to hold up that damning mirror of self-vision and have allowed me to see myself as I was: an engineer's engineer.

One key characteristic of this part of an engineer's personality is that everything in the world is seen as falling into one of two buckets: right or wrong. Oh, and another characteristic of the engineer's personality is that we'll have no problem speaking up and letting you know just exactly where we think something falls. That might be why an engineer's life is so hard.

It took me 20+ years to develop a "wrapper" to put around my engineering personality. This wrapper helped my career progress, made difficult tasks much easier, and just all around simplified my life. I was reminded just how important this evolution of my personality was today when a younger version of myself asked to talk with me.

He's involved in the electrical power generation industry and he's been having a tough time of it lately. He told me that he felt that he was just "banging his head against the wall" and that he was finding it really hard to get anything done at work.

He described himself as a "guns 'a blazing" sort of guy who feared no conversation. Read this as classic engineer talk for "I'll tell you when you're wrong." Clearly this was a social / political career crash that was just waiting to happen. What could I tell him that would help him to save himself?

The first thing that I realized is that I wasn't going to be able to help him until he wanted to be helped. Right now he just wanted to complain about how wrong everyone else was. I let him vent for a while and then asked him a few questions.

It turns out that he's had a number of projects (both work and social) that he's been the leader for. In the past, a number of them have flat out failed. This is classic engineer talk: "they just didn't get what I wanted them to do!"

Recently he did organize a successful gathering and I probed to find out more about why that one worked. It turns out that others helped him out with that one. This was a bit of an eye opener – he had not realized that he had always failed when he tried to do everything by himself.

Next we talked about that whole "guns 'a blazing" thing. He had just gotten off of a call that had started badly and he'd gone in shooting the meeting leader for not being clear about the purpose of the meeting. After he got a few shots off, he basically tuned out of the whole meeting. Clearly, this had been a showdown in the OK Corral that had turned out badly for everyone.

My big challenge here was to find a way to make him see himself as the world sees him. My first try, "what do you think the other person thought of you" didn't go very far – he was too fixated on the fact that the other guy was "wrong" to consider this. I then asked him if the call had been successful – he admitted that it had not been.

I then asked him that if it had been his assignment to make sure that the call was a success, while still playing the subordinate role that he had played, what would he have done differently? This question floored him. He didn't have an answer – an engineer hates it when he doesn't know the answer.

Having gotten his attention and partially getting him to understand that his actions had not moved the call closer to a successful ending, I then went in for the kill. I suggested that the only way to accomplish his goal of making sure that the call was successful, would have been to understand what the call leader was feeling and then persuade him to move in a direction that would make the call successful.

My young friend considered this for a bit and agreed. Hey, it's sort of like a control system problem back in school. I finished by pointing out the "guns 'a blazing" approach would never persuade anyone to move in the direction that you wanted them to move. He agreed. Now all I have to do is teach him how to be successful when interacting with others and I will have changed an engineer into a team player!

Chapter 5

Do You Want to Work With an IT Trophy Kid?

Chapter 5: Do You Want To Work With An IT Trophy Kid?

Even though the world currently looks like it is upside down, there is a much larger change going on that will have a much longer impact than this temporary financial crisis: the arrival of the millennial generation into the IT workplace. Are you ready?

Just to make sure that we're all talking about the same thing here, the millennial generation was born between 1980 and 2001. With the baby boomer generation getting ready to walk off into the sunset, the millennials are the new kids in town and they are getting ready to shake things up.

Ron Alsop who writes for the Wall Street Journal has taken some time to study what this arrival means for all of us and he's written a book with his answers in it called **The Trophy Kids Grow Up: How the Millennial Generation is Shaking Up the Workplace**. He's discovered some eye-opening things that all IT Leaders need to be aware of.

If we had to describe the millennial generation's view of work, the word that everyone seems to use is "entitled" – they want it all and they want it now. What are they asking for? How about: higher pay, flexible hours, promotions within a year, and more vacation/personal time. Why do they think that they'll get it? Studies show that nearly half of the millennials have "...*moderate to high superiority beliefs about themselves.*"

What's up with these guys / gals? Where did all of this come from? Blame it on the parents (and teachers and coaches). This is the generation that was constantly told that they were the best, the ones that got trophies even when they didn't win, and were rarely criticized in order to not damage their self-esteem. Now they are in your IT department...!

But hold on. Remember that the millennials have a solid grasp of cutting edge technology – it is a part of their life outside of work. They tend to work very well in teams and they get along well with baby boomers because they remind them so much of their own parents.

These are hard workers who will get the job done as long as an IT Leader points them in the right direction.

Chapter 6

An IT Management Nightmare: Managing Trophy Kids

Chapter 6: An IT Management Nightmare: Managing Trophy Kids

Remember that Jack Nicholson line from the movie that was made from the Steven King book "The Shining": *".. Here's Johnny..."*? I seem to recall that he delivers this line as he stands at a door with an axe in his hands trying to break into the bathroom. I suspect that many IT managers feel as though they are trapped in that bathroom and the millennial generation is on their way in.

Ron Alsop who writes for the Wall Street Journal has taken some time to study what this arrival means for all of us (hopefully no axes involved) and he's written a book with his answers in it called **The Trophy Kids Grow Up: How the Millennial Generation is Shaking Up the Workplace**. He's got some suggestions on just how to go about managing this new type of IT worker.

The first thing that needs to be realized is that the millennial generation is going to want much more attention and guidance from IT Leaders. This may come off as arrogant behavior, but it's not. The millennials got so much affirmation and positive feedback when they were growing up that when they enter the workplace they come across as being needy.

Unfortunately this need for more guidance goes hand-in-hand with the fact that millennials generally don't take suggestions for improvement very well. Blame this on their parents. IT managers are going to have to still deliver the good with the bad, but they are going to have to be careful to focus more on the good stuff.

Millennials are an interesting mix when it comes to doing work. They are used to having precise guidelines ("rules") that establish a structured situation which provides them with the order that they so desperately need.

However, at the same time millennials want a flexible work environment that allows them to balance their work and personal lives. A good way of thinking of this is that they don't view work as a place you go, rather work is something that you do.

All of this is enough to make an IT manger long for the old days when he / she was an individual contributor. However, there is an upside to all of this. The millennials have a solid grasp of cutting edge technology – it is a part of their life outside of work. They tend to work very well in teams and they get along well with baby boomers because they remind them so much of their own parents.

You've got hard workers here who will get the job done as long as an IT Leader points them in the right direction. That's why YOU are the IT Leader.

Chapter 7

Managing Trophy Kids: Can't We All Just Get Along?

Chapter 7: Managing Trophy Kids: Can't We All Just Get Along?

A lot has been written recently about the next generation of workers that is in the process of entering IT departments right now (I've done my part!) However, what's been missing is a fundamental understanding of what an IT Leader is supposed to do once they are there.

Ron Alsop who writes for the Wall Street Journal has taken some time to study what this arrival means for all of us and he's written a book with his answers in it called ***The Trophy Kids Grow Up: How the Millennial Generation is Shaking Up the Workplace***. He's got some suggestions on just how to go about managing this new type of IT worker.

One of the key differences between the millennials and the current workforce will be seen in company loyalty – it basically won't exist. The millennials have high expectations about what a company should provide them with (rapid promotions, flexible work schedules, etc.), but firms should expect very little loyalty in return.

The current economic climate notwithstanding, millennials will leave an unfulfilling job in an instant. Most firms are aware of this and retention is high on their list of issues when it comes to dealing with this generation of workers.

You might be thinking that the trophy kids will stick around for the same reasons that most of today's workers don't leave: it's scary out there without a job. However, you'd be wrong. The millennials have their parents to fall back on. They haven't burned their bridges behind them and they know that they could always move back home for a bit if things get tight.

The good news here is that the millennials have been raised to work hard. Competition is in their blood. If a job engages them, then they will be willing to work hard at it. Firms have to show these new workers that their job will end up making a difference and that the company values their work.

Chapter 8

Group Decisions Can Be the Wrong Decision for IT Leaders

Chapter 8: Group Decisions Can Be The Wrong Decision For IT Leaders

Decisions, decisions, decisions – how is an IT Leader supposed to make good ones? In our eternal quest to find a way to make good IT decisions on technologies, staff, and projects, is there **a silver bullet** that we can find that will show us the way?

One approach that is used by (too) many IT Leaders is to **follow the crowd**. I can see you shaking your head, but come on, admit it; we all like to go where everyone else is going. If you don't believe me than look around you – what development techniques are you using (agile?), what data center changes are going on (virtualization?), what initiatives are you working on (social networking?). Maybe Jason Zweig over at the Wall Street Journal can provide some insight on group decision making.

How Do Groups Make Decisions?

Group decision making is how a lot of IT decision making gets done. Robert Sutton, an organizational psychologist, over at Stanford University has spent time studying how groups make decisions. I like what he has to say – *"The best groups will be* **better** *than their best individual members and the worst groups will be* **worse** *than the worst individual."*

Sutton says that the reason that groups behave this way is because of two things. The first is that they may have a tendency to follow a given leader in sort of a rush to **conform**. The other possibility is that the group will split into **warring factions** and won't be able to reach any decisions.

How Can Groups Make GOOD Decisions?

Richard Larrick over at Duke University believes that in order for any IT group to be able to make good decisions, the IT Leader needs to have built the group correctly. Groups need to be built using people who have different **perspectives**, **experiences**, and who are **not shy** about speaking up. Of course group members also need to have those IT skills that we all value so highly: the ability to take in lots of information, filter out the important parts, and learn from any mistakes that they make.

Tips For Making Better Group Decisions

So how can an IT Leader help a group to make a good decision instead of getting tied up in knots? There's no magic cure, but here are some suggestions on what can be done to improve your odds of getting good decisions out of your groups:

- **Measure Success:** Use the collective knowledge of the group to clearly define how a decision's success should be measured. Starting at the end helps to make better decisions.

- **Use Numbers Carefully:** Groups like to use facts and statistics when making decisions. However, you need to use this kind of data to rank your options. Then the group needs to do additional research and find out what's really going on. Then create another list of ranked solutions. Average them out and you'll have a balanced decision.

- **Reframing:** When a group is charged with trying to answer a big question ("should we close our data centers"), use the power of multiple people to take both sides of the argument ("close" vs. "don't close") and have them build cases for their position. This will provide you with your best chance of seeing all sides of the question.

Final Thoughts On Group Decisions

Most IT Leaders would like to be thought of as bold decision makers who are never wrong. The reality is that **sometimes a group really is needed** in order to fully understand difficult questions. Building the group correctly and making sure that they know how to reach good decisions is part of what it takes to be a good IT Leader.

Chapter 9

Alternate Reality Games: Games That IT Leaders Know How to Play

Chapter 9: Alternate Reality Games: Games That IT Leaders Know How To Play

As an IT Leader, you've got some challenges facing you. You're managing a diverse and potentially distributed work force of highly skilled and talented IT professionals. You need to find a way to keep them challenged, and yet at the same time enable them to find ways to work together. Have you considered **Alternate Reality Games**?

Leave The Real World – Visit An Alternate Reality

As IT Leaders we have been taught that most problems can be solved with the application of some math and a whole bunch of data. However, most of us have learned that the real world is **much more complex than that** – there are a number of IT problems that can't be solved this way.

Jane McGonigal has been looking at big problems like this and she's got a solution for us: Alternate Reality Games (ARGs). ARGs are immersive games that provide a massively multi-player experience. What makes them unique (outside of their size) is that the game-play unfolds in the course of their players lives over time spans that can range from days, weeks, or even months. **This isn't your father's Wii.**

Tools Of The (Alternate Reality) Trade

Ok, I can hear you saying, so just how do you play one of these ARGs? Well, it turns out that you don't really play it – it plays you! You already probably have some hard-core gamers working on your team, so why not? The folks running the ARG show, known affectionately as "**puppet masters**" are in charge of distributing potentially thousands of pieces of information that contribute to telling the story of the ARG. These pieces for the puzzle can be distributed via websites set up for the game, email, cell phone text messages, online audio podcasts and videos, etc.

The players in the game **don't play by themselves** – there is no way that they could solve the puzzle if they did that. Instead, they need to collaborate in order to share and gain information. They do this by using social networking sites (Facebook, MySpace, etc.), wikis, chat rooms, and blogs to talk about what clues they have and what they might mean. This interaction forms the **narrative** of the game.

Sounds Like An Effort – Why Bother?

Welcome to the 21st Century. McGonigal points out that ARGs are an excellent way for IT teams to master those difficult collaboration skills that IT Leaders want them to learn. Two of the skills that she points out are **cooperation radar** – the ability to identify who can best help you, and **protovation** - the ability to prototype and test solutions quickly.

Oh, and by the way: ARGs are a lot of fun for everyone that is involved. Although they may be working through a simulation of a business problem that your firm is facing, it doesn't seem that way – **it feels like a game**.

Final Thoughts

When an IT Leader is faced with a BIG challenge that doesn't have an obvious solution, playing an ARG may be just what the CIO ordered. Although they are not easy to set up, an ARG may offer the best way to quickly test out different scenarios in **real world circumstances**.

Above and beyond the business benefits that ARGs offer, using this innovative way to stimulate and engage your team will provide you with yet another way to transform yourself from an IT manager into a **true leader**.

Chapter 10

Cheap & Easy IT Management: How to Use Social-Network Analysis to Boost Team Performance

Chapter 10: Cheap & Easy IT Management: How To Use Social-Network Analysis To Boost Team Performance

No budget, no special training, and yet you are expected to do more with less. How can you go about fixing what's wrong with your IT team during tight economic times? It turns out that there is a simple way for you to identify where you are having issues and how you can fix them. All you need to do is to learn a about a new management tool called **social-network analysis**...

It's Not Facebook

These days we're reading so much about social networks that when we hear the phrase, we automatically think of web sites like Facebook, LinkedIn, or MySpace. Well, we're not talking about those, **but there are similarities**.

Instead, what social-network mapping is all about is finding out who your team **talks with in order to solve problems and get information**. This is the type of information that everyone always knows, but never spends much time thinking about — it's basically invisible.

Once you've collected this information from your team, you will then be able to create a **social-network map** that shows the communication gaps, related information bottlenecks, and team members that are not being fully utilized.

The immediate payoff for you as an IT Leader is that you'll be able to **improve collaboration** within your team as well as perhaps uncovering some star performers that you simply didn't know about.

How About An Example?

This kind of management tool just begs for **an example**, so let's take a look at one. Let us pretend that you are an IT manager who is in charge of a team of 16 workers as shown in the following figure:

Example: You Are In Charge Of A Team Of 16 IT Workers

You create a questionnaire for your team that has only one question: "Whom do you go to in order to get answers to your technical questions?" When you get the survey forms back, you lock the door to your office and get busy creating a **social-network analysis map**. Let's say that you come up with something that looks like this:

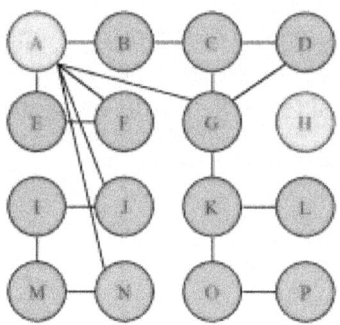

The Result Of Your Social-Network Analysis

Now you have to interpret what you've discovered. Clearly worker A is one of your star problem solvers — did you know that? It also looks like you have a hidden problem with worker H, they don't seem to be seeking help to solve problems and nobody is asking them for help. Additionally, with only a couple of exceptions, your department seems to be **divided into two groups** that really aren't talking with each other. Once again, did you know this?

For IT Leaders who are managing a team that is spread over **multiple sites**, this kind of social analysis can be even more valuable. If we sent our questionnaire out to all four sites that our team is located at, we might get the following results back.

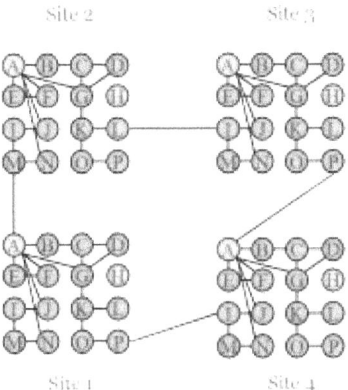

Social-Network Analysis Of Workers At Multiple Sites

What this is showing us is that although there appears to be information flowing within each of the four sites, there is very little information that flows between sites. A little more digging might reveal that the only people on your team who are talking to each other are **the managers**. If so, then you've got a problem that needs to be addressed.

What All Of This Means For You

In order to get the most value out of doing a social-network analysis, you are going to have to **carefully pick** the questions that you ask your team. One great question to include is to ask how interacting with a given team member affects the responder's energy level. This can be a good way to uncover the energy vampires on your team.

The result of making the effort to map the social structure of your IT team should product **tangible real-world payoffs**. The most valuable of these is that once you know who has the most valuable information, then you can work to make sure that everyone has easier access to that information. This should result in a decrease in the number of steps that are required to solve issues.

Ultimately understanding the **flow of communications** within your team and then taking steps to improve and facilitate it will boost your team's ability to innovate. Now that's something that we all would like to have more of!

Chapter 11

Google's Lessons For Managing Tech-Savvy Teams

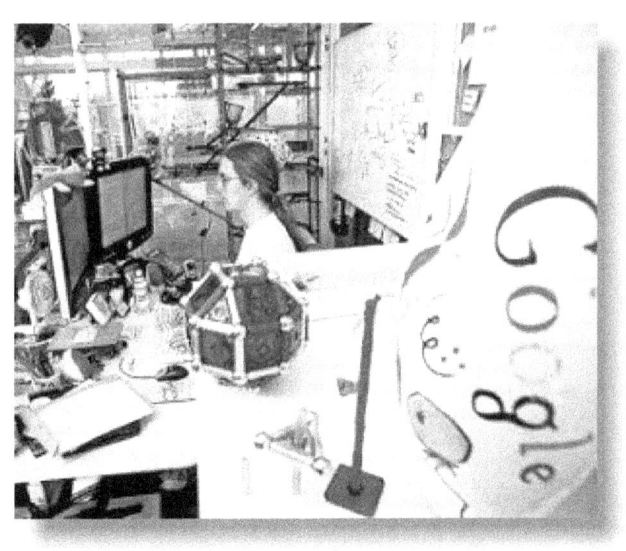

Chapter 11: Google's Lessons For Managing Tech-Savvy Teams

Sigh, if only we all could work for Google, right? If there is one company out there that seems to "get" IT, it would have to be Google. The stories that float around about how nice the Google campus is and all the free food and other perks sure make it **seem like a Shangri-La**. Hmm, but wait a minute, no matter how nice it seems, they've got to be dealing with the same IT Leader issues that we all are. Maybe it's time to have a talk with their (former) CIO...

It's All About Choice

One of the big issues that IT Leaders have to deal with on an almost constant basis is the issue of **keeping our teams up and running**. This comes down to making sure that they have the right laptops, the right operating systems, etc. If you are not careful, this can eat up a lot of your available time.

Over at Google, Douglas Merrill who was their CIO up until April of 2008 said that the model that they used for solving the individual system issue was **freedom of choice**: employees got to choose both their machine and their operating system. I'll bet that pretty much eliminates any complaining!

You would think that this would make support from an IT perspective a lot more complicated / expensive. You'd be right, but Merrill said that it didn't boost costs all that much in part because of Google's extensive use of **self-service**. They maintain internal web sites where users can go to download and install any software that they need. They do this by themselves and it places no additional burden on the IT department.

What About Security?

I can almost hear what you are saying / thinking right now: man, that must cause all sorts of **security nightmares**. Any IT Leader that you talk with these days probably has one or more horror stories about a team member downloading (or clicking on) something that they shouldn't have and causing a mess that took forever to clean up.

Merrill says that they look at things a bit differently at Google. Most companies try to secure their networks by locking down the endpoints: our laptops and our smart phones. He feels that this really doesn't work very well — thus all of the problems that we still have. At Google they put the security into **the infrastructure**.

What this means is that, yes, they still have antivirus and antispyware applications running on everyone's laptops, but they also have a lot of software running on their **corporate mail servers and infrastructure**. When taken together, they feel that they have solved the problem of just how you can secure your corporate network.

Just in case you need more convincing that they really take their security seriously, Merrill states that Google has **over 150 engineers** who work on nothing but security. They've worked very hard to make sure that security is not something that is handled by "some group" and instead is worked into everything that they do. One of the ways that they make this happen is to use automated tools to check each developer's code before it gets put into production.

What All Of This Means For You

No, most of us are not going to end up working for Google (unless they take over the world, at which this turns into a different discussion). However, **how they run their IT shop** does hold some clues for the rest of us.

When it comes to resolving issues regarding the technical environment in which their team members work, they've turned over the decision making to each employee. We can't necessarily set up the same system, but it does provide some clues. Where possible if we allow the team to decide things like what code editor to use or what template to use then all of a sudden it's not "my" decision, but rather **"our" decision** which is always a lot easier for everyone to live with.

Security is another issue that just doesn't seem to want to go away. Google's approach is to do the baseline needed at the edge of the network and then focus on **securing the core**. This just seems like an overall good idea. Additionally, setting up ways to carefully check your team's products to ensure that they are secure is always a good idea for any IT Leader.

It looks like Google is running a pretty tight ship in their IT department. Even if we can't all work there, we can still **learn from their example**…

Chapter 12

Tomorrow, Tomorrow, You'll Always Have Tomorrow – but Are You Ready?

Chapter 12: Tomorrow, Tomorrow, You'll Always Have Tomorrow – But Are You Ready?

If you've been reading the papers or watching the news on TV, you've probably started to see stories that are daring to hint at a global recovery. Now that's all fine and good and I'll believe it when it shows up. However, smart IT Leaders know that **now is the time to act**. Are you getting your team ready for the madness that will hit your firm when things really start moving once again?

Six Things That You Need To Be Doing

The thing that you've got to realize is that both you and the rest of the business have been in a hunker down, just keep the lights on mode for quite some time. The good thing about this is that everyone else in your industry has been doing the same thing. However, one-by-one everyone is going to be waking up soon and **you don't want your team to get caught unaware**.

Since you may still have a little bit of down time on your hands, now is the time to make the most of it. Here are **six things** that you need to be having your team work on now before they become too busy to think straight:

- **Simplify, Simplify, Simplify:** When we are moving at 100 mph, we have a nasty habit of creating redundant systems and duplicating processes. We do this because we don't have the time to research how things are being done right now – we just solve the same problem once again. Use this time to comb through the applications and processes that your team supports and uses and find / eliminate the duplicates.

- **Level Set:** how many user licenses are you paying for? How many of those are you using? For that matter, how well utilized are the servers and storage systems that you team uses every day? Now is the time to sort all of this out. Get rid of the licenses that you don't need any more and make sure that you are maximizing the value from each one of your hardware resources.

- **Call In The Governance:** When things start to pick up, everybody and their mother's Uncle are going to be coming to your team and asking you to do work for them. Now is the time to lay down the law on how you'll be approving what projects you'll be working on.

- **Inventory Skill Sets:** If you look out into the future 12 months or so, what skills will your team need to be able to bring to the table to do the work that will be asked of them? Now is the time to bring in people who have the needed skills or to send your team off to get some training.

- **What's Your Value?:** This is something that you should have done a long time ago; however, if you haven't then you need to do it now. You need to sit down with your team and make sure that everyone has a clear understanding of how your team supports the rest of the business.

- **Learn To Live With Uncertainty:** As IT professionals we love it when things are cut & dried; however, that's not the way that life works. It's great to start out with a plan but the reality is that things will happen and the plan will need to be changed. How it gets changed and how the new plan gets communicated will be key to your team's success going forward.

What All Of This Means For You

The Chinese curse says "May you live in interesting times" – and we certainly are. However, as busy as we are today, it's starting to look like we are going to be getting a lot busier as the global economy **starts to pick up**.

Sharp IT Leaders realize that this is the time that we need to be working with our team to work through those issues that we can get put right before we get busy. **Time invested now will pay dividends later**.

The difference between being an IT manager and an IT Leader is that you take the time to look into the future and **you prepare for it before it happens**. Do this and you'll be able to show your team the way to go...

It's from the forge of failure that the steel of success is formed.

Hard Work Does Not Guarantee Success, But Success Does Not Happen Without Hard Work.

— Dr. Jim Anderson

Create IT Departments That Are Productive And A Valuable Asset To The Rest Of The Company !

Dr. Jim Anderson is available to provide training and coaching on the topics that are the most important to people who have to manage IT departments: how can I build a productive IT department (and keep it together) while at the same time providing the rest of the company with the IT services that they need?

Dr. Anderson believes that in order to both learn and remember what he says, speakers need to laugh. Each one of his speeches is full of fun and humor so that what he says "sticks" with everyone.

Dr. Anderson's CIO SkillsTraining Includes:

1. How to identify and attract the right type of IT workers to your IT department.
2. How to build relationships with the company's senior management in order to get the support that you need?
3. How to stay on top of changing technology and security issues so that you never get surprised?

Dr. Jim Anderson works with over 100 customers per year. To invite Dr. Anderson to work with you, contact him at:

Phone: 813-418-6970 or
Email: jim@BlueElephantConsulting.com

Blue Elephant Consulting

Speaking.   Negotiating.   Managing.   Marketing

Photo Credits:

Cover - By: Invoke
http://www.flickr.com/photos/invokemedia/

Chapter 1 - By: Sergio Russo
https://www.flickr.com/photos/xcbiker/

Chapter 2 – By Venessa Miemis
https://www.flickr.com/photos/venessamiemis/

Chapter 3 - By: Eneas de Troya
https://www.flickr.com/photos/eneas/

Chapter 4 - By: Ol.v!er [H2vPk]
http://www.flickr.com/photos/smallbox/

Chapter 5 - By: Lance Page
https://www.flickr.com/photos/truthout/

Chapter 6 - By: Brad.K
https://www.flickr.com/photos/stopbits/

Chapter 7 - By: Andy Simmonds
https://www.flickr.com/photos/andyrs/

Chapter 8 - By: SalFalko
http://www.flickr.com/photos/safari_vacation/

Chapter 9 - By: plantronicsgermany
http://www.flickr.com/photos/plantronicsgermany/

Chapter 10 - By: Kusumsiri Wiajayratna
http://www.flickr.com/photos/kusumsiri/

Chapter 11 - By: TopRank Online Marketing
http://www.flickr.com/photos/toprankblog/

Chapter 12 - By: Miriam
http://www.flickr.com/photos/45617397@N05/

Other Books By The Author

Product Management

- Product Management Secrets: Techniques For Product Managers To Boost Product Sales And Increase Customer Satisfaction

- Product Development Lessons For Product Managers: How Product Managers Can Create Successful Products

- Customer Lessons For Product Managers: Techniques For Product Managers To Better Understand What Their Customers Really Want

- Product Failure Lessons For Product Managers: Examples Of Products That Have Failed For Product Managers To Learn From

- Communication Skills For Product Managers: The Communication Skills That Product Managers Need To Know How To Use In Order To Have A Successful Product

- How To Have A Successful Product Manager Career: The Things That You Need To Be Doing TODAY In Order To Have A Successful Product Manager Career

- Product Manager Product Success: How to keep your product on track and make it become a success

Public Speaking

- How To Become A Better Speaker By Changing How You Speak: Change techniques that will transform a speech into a memorable event

- How To Give A Great Presentation: Presentation techniques that will transform a speech into a memorable event

- How To Rehearse In Order To Give The Perfect Speech: How to effectively rehearse your next speech to that your message be remembered forever!

- Secrets To Creating The Perfect Speech: How to create a speech that will make your message be remembered forever!

- Secrets To Organizing The Perfect Speech: How to organize the best speech of your life!

- Secrets To Planning The Perfect Speech: How to plan to give the best speech of your life

- How To Show What You Mean During A Presentation: How to use visual techniques to transform a speech into a memorable event

CIO Skills

- How CIOs Can Solve The Security Puzzle: Tips And Techniques For CIOs To Use In Order To Secure Both Their IT Department And Their Company

- What CIOs Need To Know About Working With Partners: Techniques For CIOs To Use In Order To Be Able To Successfully Work With Partners

- Critical CIO Management Skills: Decision Making Skills That Every CIO Needs To Have In Order To Be Able To Make The Right Choices

- How CIOs Can Make Innovation Happen: Tips And Techniques For CIOs To Use In Order To Make Innovation Happen In Their IT Department

- CIO Communication Skills Secrets: Tips And Techniques For CIOs To Use In Order To Become Better Communicators

- Managing Your CIO Career: Steps That CIOs Have To Take In Order To Have A Long And Successful Career

- CIO Business Skills: How CIOs can work effectively with the rest of the company!

IT Manager Skills

- How IT Managers Can Make Innovation Happen: Tips And Techniques For IT Managers To Use In Order To Make Innovation Happen In Their Teams

- Staffing Skills IT Managers Must Have: Tips And Techniques That IT Managers Can Use In Order To Correctly Staff Their Teams

- Secrets Of Effective Leadership For IT Managers: Tips And Techniques That IT Managers Can Use In Order To Develop Leadership Skills

- IT Manager Career Secrets: Tips And Techniques That IT Managers Can Use In Order To Have A Successful Career

- IT Manager Budgeting Skills: How IT Managers Can Request, Manage, Use, And Track Their Funding

Negotiating

- Learn How To Signal In Your Next Negotiation: How To Develop The Skill Of Effective Signaling In A Negotiation In Order To Get The Best Possible Outcome

- Learn The Skill Of Exploring In A Negotiation: How To Develop The Skill Of Exploring What Is Possible In A Negotiation In Order To Reach The Best Possible Deal

- Learn How To Argue In Your Next Negotiation: How To Develop The Skill Of Effective Arguing In A Negotiation In Order To Get The Best Possible Outcome

- How To Open Your Next Negotiation: How To Start A Negotiation In Order To Get The Best Possible Outcome

- Preparing For Your Next Negotiation: What You Need To Do BEFORE A Negotiation Starts In Order To Get The Best Possible Deal

"Tips And Techniques That IT Managers Can Use In Order To Develop Productive Teams"

> This book has been written with one goal in mind – to show you how an IT manager can build high performance teams. It's not easy being an IT manager so we're going to show you what you need to be doing in order create teams that can work together and deliver results!
>
> **Let's Make Your IT Career A Success!**

What You'll Find Inside:

- **HOW CAN AN IT LEADER CHANGE AN ENGINEER INTO A TEAM PLAYER?**

- **AN IT MANAGEMENT NIGHTMARE: MANAGING TROPHY KIDS**

- **CHEAP & EASY IT MANAGEMENT: HOW TO USE SOCIAL-NETWORK ANALYSIS TO BOOST TEAM PERFORMANCE**

- **GOOGLE'S LESSONS FOR MANAGING TECH-SAVVY TEAMS**

Dr. Jim Anderson brings his 25 years of real-world experience to this book. He's been an IT manager at some of the world's largest firms. He's going to show you what you need to do (and not do!) in order to successfully manage your career!

www.ingramcontent.com/pod-product-compliance
Lightning Source LLC
Chambersburg PA
CBHW071807170526
45167CB00003B/1211